# MAJOR DI-
# AMONDS
# NIGHTS
# &KNIVES

Also by Katie Foster:
Animal Problems (2015)

# MAJOR DI-AMONDS NIGHTS &KNIVES

By Katie Foster

Trident Press
Boulder, CO

Copyright © 2018 by Katie Foster

All rights reserved. No part of this book may be reproduced in any form or by any electronic or mechanical means, including information storage and retrieval systems, without permission in writing from the publisher, except for review.

Published by Trident Press
940 Pearl St., Boulder, CO 80302

ISBN: 978-0-9992499-1-8

For the ghost in Philly who brought this story to me.

# MAJOR

# 0

And how the egg contains the kernel of death. Folded into it. Building an exterior against death. Herded into existence, the small white animal nipping at the heels. Motion toward essential form. The egg begins to be a beginning. Neither blessed golden moment nor total dark. Somewhere inside. Could go anywhere you know.

# I

All the ingredients on the table. He raised his hand to the light. Red supple wool fell he shed his clothes. Filled me. Pointed to the earth and said, "There, the birth." Set in motion a series of happenings cannot be taken back. Magic given into the world does not return until fulfilled.

## II

I sit between the pillars filling space. Feeling an opening of space as I enact around me a stillness, quickening. Hands tucked into folds of gut, flesh seated. I close my eyes and feel the moon on me. It is happening now.

## III

Blooming. I am clothed in silk roses. Belly swelling. The wheat is getting tall again. Life crowns me with the giving of it. My pillows, pink and orange, welcome me into the recline of a woman full of something as of yet undisclosed.

## IV

My father does not know.
Sits like stone. Hands like
rams staring down from
the mountain. Not going anywhere, certainly
not getting down. His
advancing age at odds
with what is coming.
Coming to be known.

## V

The midwife I meet with in secret treats me coldly. She matches her grey eyes in tone. She too raises a hand from red robes but points nowhere. Consults my body as a matter of course. Duty doled. She sees into me and says nothing but, "Eat fruit and sleep. Clementines, tangerines, any citrus will do."

## VI

I meet him in the garden at dawn. "Is it happening?" "It is," I affirm. I undress so he may see. We stand apart. He takes me in. Beneath the lemon tree he sees what I have known. And dawn finds us and breaks over us a sea.

# VII

Sick of motion. The slightest change in direction lands a peach pit in my stomach, my throat. A decreasing tolerance for lurching forward. I want to be still. Bring me to a settled place stuck in place enough enough I too am jostled into being. The way a top spins without wings.

## VIII

I have come to understand what is inside me is a monster. I feed roses onto its terrible tongue. It has an orange hide and claws made for ripping. I can yes I can feel it snaring claws into my side. And I bear it.

## IX

To carry forth the light.
To retreat upon the silent
snow. A staff to guide to
lean to stumble upon. My
way is known but it is dark.
I feel a path into the night.

# X

The devil, the angels, the snakes have decided. The ram with spiraled horns – it has decided. The griffin, thumb holding his place on the page, has decided. And the ox and the shield, they decided. I am going to die and my child is going to die.

## XI

Between the pillars again I
understand what is about
to be done. My sentence
written. Not in stone but
the kernel of death inside
me sprouting. Raising
sword despite the yellow
day. Here I am caught in
the balance of nearly –

## XII

My child hangs in me upside down, right ankle behind left knee. Head rushing to be filled with blood I gave it. And as he hangs he turns to stone. A blue face. Cracked lips. Bulging eyes, closed, dying to escape their lids. To escape me.

## XIII

So I gave the world a death and left at once. The child split me, simply. I offered my gift and my gift was in itself entirely consumed, as was I. The water poured forth with blood. And I knew the black flag waving on the horizon was for me to follow.

## XIV

The first thing about being dead is it is not quiet. Rushing water and beating wings come close. A roar without a mouth. And the virtue of death is that of changing one to another.

## XV

I see the devil in his chains. "Are you hungry" "I am not" "Do you desire" "Only to be free" "My teeth are broken shards ground to dust yours too shall be" "I already have blood running down my leg" "That is your way in to where you will rest."

## XVI

And with these words
an unsettling motion
underfoot, giving way,
buckling into nothing.
And I fell from the tow-
er of the dead head first,
arms outstretched, cry-
ing out for my life and
my child. No end in sight.

## XVII

I land in the garden of
my naked form. It is familiar as a dream. My
impulse is to fill the jug
with water, empty it, fill
it again. This gesture, I
know, means something
but I cannot remember,
transfixed by the vessel.

## XVIII

The light rises on the edge of the garden, perched between two pillars. This framing leaves me feeling pictured – dislocated from the world in a layer of transparent image. Where does my body stop. Where does the light begin. The dogs regard the light with bared teeth.

## XIX

My child rides a white horse over the horizon. The sun announces the presence of his possibility. He is free and roaming and I watch him part the field of sunflowers turning to greet him. But I cannot catch up. The horse outpaces me tenfold and I am stuck in the garden reaching ever after.

## XX

I raise my blue hands to heaven. A trumpet calls. And a voice comes over the water rolling in with a wave. "Here you are. In between. May you find peace, pleasure, mud."

## XXI

And the world holds me
in the arms of my death.
My monster approves.
The man, the ram, the
snaking water are behold-
en, beloved in my no-lon-
ger-being. I have come
into the world as I left
it: hands full of magic.

# DIAMONDS

◊

Red cloth.

◊ ◊

Red cloth.
    Milk.

Red cloth.
Milk.
Needles.

◊ ◊ ◊ ◊

Red cloth.
      Milk.
Needles.
Bone saw.

>            Red cloth.
>                    Milk.
>                    Needles.
> Bone saw.
> Spoon.

◊ ◊ ◊ ◊ ◊ ◊

Red cloth.
        Milk.
Needles.
      Bone saw.
     Spoon.
Toy soldier.

◊ ◊ ◊ ◊ ◊ ◊ ◊

Red cloth.
    Milk.
Needles.
    Bone saw.
  Spoon.
    Toy soldier.
    Matches.

◊ ◊ ◊ ◊ ◊ ◊ ◊

      Red cloth.
            Milk.
    Needles.
          Bone saw.
      Spoon.
         Toy soldier.
         Matches.
Rope.

◊ ◊ ◊ ◊ ◊ ◊ ◊ ◊

Red cloth.
        Milk.
    Needles.
        Bone saw.
      Spoon.
        Toy soldier.
      Matches.
           Rope.
        Locket.

                    Red cloth.
          Milk.
       Needles.
            Bone saw.
         Spoon.
              Toy soldier.
            Matches.
                    Rope.
                  Locket.
Lost.

# NIGHTS

●

ever            fearing
heart of light. Mother

• •

of      mercy,    make
a    bed    for    my
sleep  that  will  not

●  ●  ●

stop   to   sleep.   Love
as   strong   as   death.
Deep                quiet

● ● ● ●

of      the     earth    to
quiet     you.     Asleep
in     the     arms     of

● ● ● ● ●

love   and   dust.   Those
wild   plunging   animals,
n      a      m      e      s

● ● ● ● ● ●

unknown. The earth
gapes open and light
goes down deep

● ● ● ● ● ● ●

to    those   who    blink
in      terror    at     it.
I        told         you

● ● ● ● ● ● ● ●

everything   in the dark.
At     the    bottom   of
the                    belly

● ● ● ● ● ● ● ● ●

of the cave I drew
a shape as quick
as I could muster.

● ● ● ● ● ● ● ● ● ●

A single gesture. And woke to the sound of the light.

# KNIVES

†

the blade, drawing
                    blood

† †

in the shape
of  a  body  beginning
      to        disappear

† † †

hold steady severing
      is delicate work
flesh
      resists, hoping to
remain

†††† 

in a dream the knife is
stuck
    in a wall and I
squeeze it
    for milk
    it milks

††††† 

the blade hidden
        underfoot  in  tall
grass

a prick     a fleck
    of spit on the
wound
    the taste of my
own
    salt

††††††

in my belly      m    y
eyes
      puncture

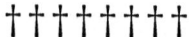

it holds open a human
space

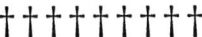

    is wet        is warm

and the milk is sweet
   gold as the hilt
   wide open

Katie Foster is a poet and artist in Providence, Rhode Island, where she is completing her MFA in Literary Arts at Brown University. She has vivid dreams.

# Other Fine Titles from Trident Press:

*Blood-Soaked Buddha/Hard Earth Pascal*
by Noah Cicero

"Far too many books about Buddhism get bogged down in scholarly double-speak. Others are full of far-fetched fantasies. Noah's book isn't like that. It's a real book for real people."
*Brad Warner, author of* Hardcore Zen

*it gets cold*
by j.avery

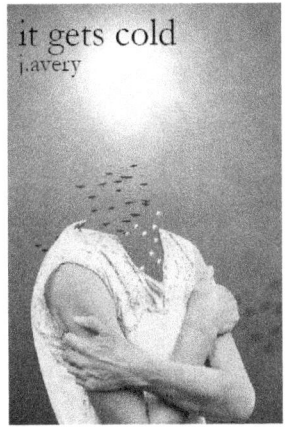

*it gets cold* demands a body that is both the haunting and the house, a queerness that is both living and dying. What can be gained by inhabiting this liminal space? What can the inhabitation of dying bring to the living? What can be done when it gets cold?

www.ingramcontent.com/pod-product-compliance
Lightning Source LLC
Chambersburg PA
CBHW052134010526
44113CB00036B/2259